Food

BANANAS

Louise Spilsbury

www.heinemann.co.uk/library
Visit our website to find out more information about Heinemann Library books.

To order:
☎ Phone 44 (0) 1865 888066
🖹 Send a fax to 44 (0) 1865 314091
🖥 Visit the Heinemann Bookshop at www.heinemann.co.uk/library to browse our catalogue and order online.

First published in Great Britain by Heinemann Library,
Halley Court, Jordan Hill, Oxford OX2 8EJ
a division of Reed Educational and Professional Publishing Ltd.
Heinemann is a registered trademark of Reed Educational and Professional Publishing Ltd.

OXFORD MELBOURNE AUCKLAND
JOHANNESBURG BLANTYRE GABORONE
IBADAN PORTSMOUTH (NH) USA CHICAGO

Designed by Celia Floyd
Illustrated by Alan Fraser and Jeff Edwards
Originated by Ambassador Litho Ltd
Printed in Hong Kong/China by South China Printing Co.

ISBN 0 431 12770 0 (hardback)
06 05 04 03 02
10 9 8 7 6 5 4 3 2 1

British Library Cataloguing in Publication Data
Spilsbury, Louise
    Bananas. – (Food)
    1. Bananas 2. Juvenile literature
    I. Title
    641.3'4772

Acknowledgements
The Publishers would like to thank the following for permission to reproduce photographs:
Ardea London: David Dixon, p.13, Liz Bomford, p.12; Corbis: pp.4, 9, 11, 14, 15, 16, 17, 18, 19, 25; Garden and Wildlife Matters: p.20; Gareth Boden: p.22; Holt Studios International: pp.5, 21; Liz Eddison: pp.23, 28, 29 (top and bottom); Oxford Scientific Films: Richard Davies, p.8; Photodisc: p.6; Stone: p.24; Visuals Unlimited: Jack Ballard, p.7.

Cover photograph reproduced with permission of Gareth Boden.

Every effort has been made to contact copyright holders of any material reproduced in this book.
Any omissions will be rectified in subsequent printings if notice is given to the Publishers.

CONTENTS

Words written in bold, **like this**, are explained in the Glossary.

WHAT ARE BANANAS?

Bananas are a kind of **fruit** that we can eat. A fruit is a part of a plant. Bananas are one of the most popular fruits in the world.

Bananas do not grow on trees. They grow on banana plants. Farmers grow lots of banana plants together in **plantations**, like this.

KINDS OF BANANAS

There are hundreds of different kinds of bananas in the world. The kind we usually see in shops is the common yellow banana.

Other kinds of bananas look and taste different. They may be different colours, shapes and sizes. Plantains are a banana you cook before eating.

IN THE PAST

The first banana plants grew in Malaysia more than 4000 years ago. Many different kinds of bananas still grow in Malaysia today.

Lots of the bananas we eat today come from the Caribbean. Spanish **explorers** first grew banana plants there 500 years ago.

AROUND THE WORLD

Bananas grow in **tropical** countries where it is sunny and it rains a lot. This map of the world shows you where most banana plants grow.

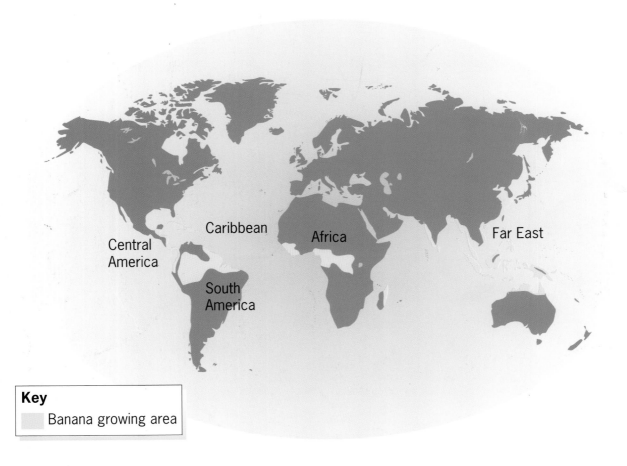

Central
America

Caribbean

Africa

Far East

South
America

Key
Banana growing area

Some people use the leaves of the banana plant, as well as eating the **fruit**. In China people use the leaves to make mats, to cover roofs and to wrap food.

BANANA PLANTS

Banana plants grow from an underground **stem**. Long leaves grow up from the stem. The bases of the leaves grow so tightly together they look like a **tree trunk**.

leaves

base of the leaves

Bananas grow from a huge **stalk** of flowers. This comes from the middle of the plant. Farmers call bananas 'fingers'. They call the bunches 'hands'.

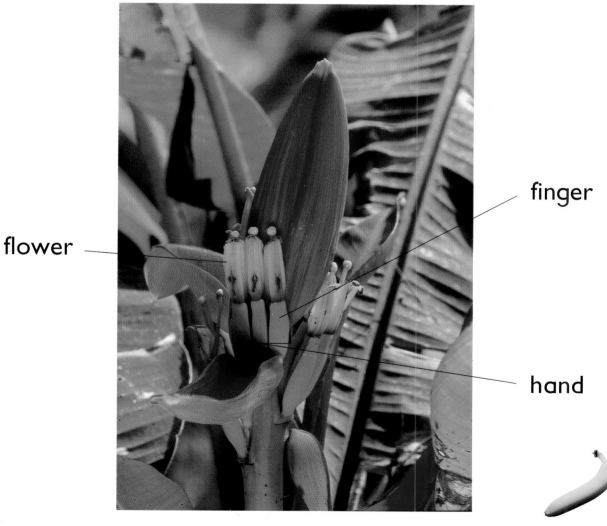

flower

finger

hand

GROWING BANANAS

In some places, workers put big plastic bags over the tiny bananas. This stops birds and insects from eating them.

Some people feed their banana plants with **fertilizers** to help them grow well. People also use sprays to stop the plants getting **diseases**.

PICKING AND WASHING

Bananas take about three months to grow. Workers pick them before they are **ripe**, when they are still green. They cut the whole **stalk** off the plant.

Then workers cut the green bananas into bunches. They wash the bananas in huge baths of cold water. This cleans any dirt off the **fruits**.

SORTING AND PACKING

Workers check the bananas and throw away any damaged ones. Stickers on each banana tell **consumers** where they come from.

Workers pack the bananas into
boxes. These boxes stop the bananas
from being damaged while they travel
from the **plantation** to the shops.

19

BANANAS TO US

Some bananas are sold in the country where they grew. Others are **exported** to different countries. They travel on ships in containers like giant fridges to keep them fresh.

Before bananas go to the shops, they go to a ripening centre. This has warm rooms that make the bananas **ripe**. Bananas turn yellow when ripe.

EATING BANANAS

Most people eat bananas **raw** (uncooked). You just take off the **peel** and eat the **fruit** inside. Some people like to eat sliced banana with cereal.

Bananas also taste good made into muffins, cakes, breads or yoghurt. You can buy banana **products**, such as banana chips or **dried** bananas.

GOOD FOR YOU

Bananas are good for you. They contain **vitamins**. Vitamins help your body to grow and protect you from **disease**.

Bananas contain **carbohydrates** too. Carbohydrates help to fill you up and give you lots of energy. Runners often eat bananas to keep them going in a long race.

HEALTHY EATING

You need to eat different kinds of food to keep you well. This food pyramid shows you how much of each different food you need.

You should eat some of the things at the bottom and in the middle of the pyramid every day. Sweet foods are at the top of the pyramid. Try not to eat too many of these!

The food in each part of the pyramid helps your body in different ways.

Bananas belong in the middle of the pyramid.

Cakes, sweets, **fats**, oils and honey

Milk, yoghurt and cheese

Meat, fish, eggs and nuts

Vegetables

Fruit

Bread, **cereals**, rice and pasta

27

BANANA MILKSHAKE RECIPE

1 Take the banana out of its **peel** and put it into a blender (mixer).

2 Add a cup of milk, 3 scoops of vanilla ice-cream and a teaspoon of lemon juice.

You will need:
- 1 banana
- 1 cup of milk
- 3 scoops of vanilla ice-cream
- 1 teaspoon of lemon juice

Ask an adult to help you!

3 Put the lid onto the blender and ask an adult to turn it on for 1 minute.

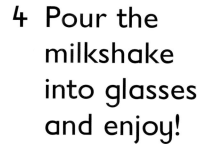

4 Pour the milkshake into glasses and enjoy!

GLOSSARY

carbohydrate kind of food that gives us energy

cereals grains like wheat and rice that are used to make foods like flour, bread and breakfast cereals

consumers people who buy things they need or want, like food

disease diseases can harm people, other animals and plants. If a plant gets a disease, it may mean its fruit is not good to eat.

dried some foods are dried before being packed and sold. They can be kept for a long time before people use them.

explorers people who travelled around the world. They were looking for lands that people from their own countries had never visited before.

exported when a product is grown or made in one country but taken to another country to be sold

fat type of food. Butter oil and margarine are kinds of fat. It is not healthy to eat or drink too many fatty foods.

fertilizers sprays or powders that help plants grow bigger and produce more fruit

fruit part of a plant that we can eat. Fruits include apples, oranges, bananas and grapes.

peel outer layer or 'skin' of a fruit

plantation place where lots of banana plants grow together

products things that are made to be sold

raw not cooked

ripe when a fruit is ready to eat

stalk part of a plant from which flowers grow

stem part of plant that holds leaves and flowers up above the ground

tree trunk large woody stem of a tree

tropical certain countries which are very hot and sunny. They get lots of rain and they never have frost in winter.

vitamin kind of goodness that is in certain foods. Vitamins help you grow and keep healthy.

MORE BOOKS TO READ

Plants: Flowers, Fruits and Seeds, Angela Royston, Heinemann Library, 1999

Safe and Sound: Eat Well, Angela Royston, Heinemann Library, 1999

Senses: Tasting, Karen Hartley, Chris Macro, Phillip Taylor, Heinemann Library, 2000

The Senses: Taste, Mandy Suhr, Hodder Wayland, 1994

INDEX

Titles in the *Food* series include:

Hardback   0 431 12770 0

Hardback   0 431 12700 X

Hardback   0 431 12771 9

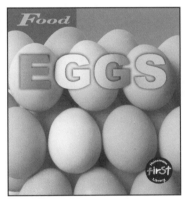

Hardback   0 431 12702 6

Hardback   0 431 12706 9

Hardback   0 431 12701 8

Hardback   0 431 12772 7

Hardback   0 431 12773 5

Find out about the other titles in this series on our website www.heinemann.co.uk/library